FRANK LLOYD WRIGHT

FRANK LLOYD WRIGHT

SPENCER HART

BARNES
&NOBLE
BOOKS
NEW YORK

This edition published by
Barnes & Noble, Inc.,
by arrangement with Brompton Books Corporation.

Produced by Brompton Books Corporation
15 Sherwood Place
Greenwich, CT 06830

ISBN 1-56619-184-X

Printed in China

Reprinted 1994, 1995, 1996, 1999

PAGE 1: *Frank Lloyd Wright, c. 1904.*

PAGE 2: *Frank Wright Thomas House, 1901*
(The Harem)
Oak Park, Illinois
Photo: © Steinkamp/Ballogg Chicago

CONTENTS

FRANK LLOYD WRIGHT: AN EVOLVING ARCHITECTURE

Frank Lloyd Wright's career as an architect began in 1887, when he was twenty years old, and lasted until his death in 1959 – a period of seventy-two years. But longevity alone does not account for the insistently evolutionary quality of his work. This was also, and perhaps primarily, the result of his restless temperament, which saw each new project as a struggle for synthesis on its own unique terms. The unity Wright achieved in his most successful buildings was unrepeatable. He had to work to achieve it again and again. In the process, even disappointments and failures were caught up and incorporated into new forms of expression. His prodigious talent and capacity for work carried him through personal and professional crises to renewed enthusiasm, heightened sensibilities, and an unflagging sense of what could be realized in "the next one" – his invariable answer to the question, "What is your favorite or most important project?"

The man who became the best-known and most influential American architect of our times was a midwesterner born and bred. His mother, Anna Lloyd Jones, came from a prosperous farming family of Welsh ancestry that had settled in rural Spring Green, Wisconsin. She was a schoolteacher who married a music teacher, William Cary Wright, after he was widowed by the death of his first wife, Permilia Holcomb. Wright had come west from New England after studying law at Amherst College and made his living as a traveling Baptist minister and music teacher. He was an intelligent and attractive man of forty-six, the father of four children by his first marriage, when he married the twenty-nine-year-old schoolteacher who had been a boarder at his home before his wife's death.

The Lloyd Joneses were Unitarians and doubtful about Wright's Baptist background, but Anna was a strong-minded and demanding woman who had seemed unlikely ever to marry. Grudgingly, they accepted the transplanted New Englander into the family circle at Spring Green, which irreverent neighbors referred to as "the valley of the God-Almighty Joneses." Frank Lloyd Wright was born to this union on June 8, 1867, in Richland Center, Wisconsin. A slender handsome child, intense by nature, he was idolized by his mother from the first.

In 1874 William Cary Wright relocated his family to Weymouth, Massachusetts, where he assumed the pastorate of a small Baptist church. Two years later, the family traveled to Philadelphia for the historic Centennial Exposition. According to Wright's autobiography, first published in 1932,

ABOVE: *Young Frank Lloyd Wright in 1889, at the age of 22. Two years earlier, Wright began working as a draftsman for the firm of Adler and Sullivan.*

OPPOSITE: *Frank Lloyd Wright in 1958, displaying a model of a prefabricated house. In designing houses that could in large part be factory-built, Wright said he was simply converting the machine into an artist's tool.*

this is where his mother learned about the theories of German educator Frie-drich W. A. Froebel, creator of the kindergarten system. Early-childhood education was deeply influenced by Froebel, whose methods included the use of colorful geometric shapes as construction toys. It is widely assumed that Wright's future career was affected by his introduction to Froebel's methods. Like her sisters, Jane and Nell Lloyd Jones, who founded the progressive Hill-side Home School in Spring Green, Anna's interest in education was lifelong, and its major focus was her son. This remained true even after the birth of her daughters, Jane and Maginel (a diminutive of Margaret Ellen).

In 1877 the Wrights moved back to Wisconsin, where they settled in Madison, the state capital. Their marriage was deeply troubled, and their son was drawn to his mother's side in the growing conflict between his parents. His autobiography shows that he effectively repudiated his father, who left home in 1885. That year, the eighteen-year-old Wright was apprenticed to a Madison builder, Allan D. Conover, who was also the dean of engineering at the University of Wisconsin. For two years, Wright attended classes in drafts-manship, for which he showed remarkable aptitude, and got practical build-ing experience in Conover's office.

In 1887 the aspiring architect left the restrictive atmosphere of his home for the wider world of Chicago, then expanding and still rebuilding after the great fire of 1871. Architectural opportunity had attracted many notable designers from the East Coast, including Henry Hobson Richardson and Joseph Lyman Silsbee, to whom Wright applied for work as a draftsman. Silsbee had been retained by Wright's uncle, the Reverend Jenkin Lloyd Jones, to design a new building for his congregation at All Souls' Church. Wright spent some months working for Silsbee and was influenced by his informal "Shingle-style" architecture, with its asymmetrical elements derived partly from the work of Norman Shaw and other British architects. Like them, Wright was influenced by English critic and social theorist John Ruskin and impressed by the Arts and Crafts movement in Great Britain and Europe. He had already taken the anticlassical stance that he would maintain throughout his career.

In the fall of 1887 Wright applied for a job as a draftsman with the rapidly growing firm of Adler and Sullivan, which was doing innovative work in which he found much to admire. Louis Sullivan, then only thirty-one years old and the creative half of the partnership, had a gift for reinterpreting

LEFT: *Henry Hobson Richardson (1838-1886), an eminent architect in his day, went west to Chicago after the great fire of 1871, to take advantage of the architectural opportunities available there.*

BELOW LEFT: *Louis Henri Sullivan (1856-1924), one of America's most innovative designers. Sullivan became Wright's mentor during Wright's six-year tenure with Adler and Sullivan.*

OPPOSITE: *Hillside Home School II, in Spring Green, Wisconsin. Wright designed the building in 1901 for his aunts Nell and Jane Lloyd Jones. With the establishment of the Taliesin Fellowship in 1933, the school became part of the Taliesin complex.*

traditional styles in a fresh new way that he saw as essential for architectural relevance in a changing society. He had an aversion to urban life as it was lived in the crowded, dirty, unplanned cities of the time, and to high-rise buildings that dwarfed the people who lived and worked in them.

During Wright's six-year tenure with Adler and Sullivan, Louis Sullivan created the first truly modern skyscraper: the Wainwright Building in St. Louis, Missouri. Here, the slender brick piers that rise between the windows and at the building's corners clearly express the steel skeleton beneath them; it is clear that the walls are not self-sustaining masses of brick, as in the traditional post-and-beam construction of the earliest high-rise buildings. When Sullivan said that "form follows function," he implied a flexible relationship between inner and outer space. His gift for naturalistic decorative design made his commercial architecture even more distinctive. It was expressed most extravagantly in the great portal created for the Transportation Building at the World's Columbian Exposition held in Chicago in 1893. Wright worked on this project (the Golden Door) and many others. In fact, he was handling most of the firm's residential commissions. He had signed a five-year contract with Adler and Sullivan in 1889 and become an important part of its practice. However, a dispute about commissions undertaken by Wright on his own time led to a breach with Sullivan in 1893, and Wright went his own way.

By this time Wright had married his first wife, Catherine Tobin, and fathered the first of their six children. He had designed a house in the suburb of Oak Park, Illinois, and had built it with money advanced by Sullivan. During the mid-1890s, he maintained an office in Chicago's Steinway Hall with several other young architects, but as he became better known and received new commissions – many from his neighbors in Oak Park – he did more and more work at home. This became increasingly difficult as his family grew, and in the late 1890s, he built a separate studio. A group of young assistants and an office manager, Isabel Roberts, were constantly occupied with the work that flowed into the little complex.

The house and studio at Oak Park became a laboratory for Wright's design experiments from 1889 until 1909. Both buildings were in a constant state of renovation, expansion, and rearrangement – a process that would continue throughout his life with future homes that became architectural landmarks, including Taliesin in Spring Green, Wisconsin, and Taliesin West in Scottsdale, Arizona. It was at Oak Park that Wright created his first

OPPOSITE: *Louis Sullivan's Wainwright Building in St. Louis, Missouri, the first modern skyscraper.*

RIGHT: *Frank Lloyd Wright and his family assembled on the steps of his Oak Park home. They are, from left, Uncle Jenkin Lloyd Jones, Aunt Susan, sister Jane, wife Catherine holding son Lloyd, mother Anna Lloyd Wright, sister Maginel, Frank Lloyd Wright and cousin Mary.*

RIGHT: *The Transportation Building at the World's Columbian Exposition held in Chicago in 1893. Wright worked with Sullivan on this project.*

top-lighted, open workspace in the studio and designed the furniture and fit-
tings, which he considered integral to every structure. His ideas on the relationship between the Arts and Crafts movement and the machine age were
taken seriously and came to life in such designs as the William Winslow House
in River Forest, Illinois. This precursor of the Prairie House exemplifies
Wright's objectives in residential architecture: large, free-flowing living areas,
well lighted by windows that opened the house to continuous views of the
grounds; fireplaces that defined the various living areas and served as focal
points for family life; furnishings designed specifically for the house and the
needs of its occupants and crafted with respect to the beauty of natural
materials; and plantings and outdoor fixtures designed for a harmonious sense
of unity between site and dwelling.

Wright dismissed the concept of the house as a box subdivided into
smaller boxes and eventually eliminated both basement and attic. Servants'
quarters were moved to the kitchen area, which was well ventilated to provide
an odorless and sanitary working environment. He replaced the traditional
sashed window with casement windows, which opened outward and increased the sense of continuity between indoors and natural surroundings.
Second floors were often lighted by continuous bands of clerestory windows,
overhung by light-colored eaves that extended protectively from a low-
hipped roof. The sense of shelter was paramount, and his houses were
typically horizontal, rather than vertical, laid out on a cruciform plan. These
features are seen in many designs of the late 1890s and early 1900s, including
the Isidore Heller House in Chicago, the Joseph Husser House overlooking
Lake Michigan, and the William G. Fricke and Frank Wright Thomas houses
in Oak Park.

Wright's views on contemporary architecture first received national
attention in 1901, when the Curtis Publishing Company commissioned
several designs for publication in the *Ladies' Home Journal*. The innovative
houses Wright designed included "A Home in a Prairie Town," to be constructed at a cost of $7,000, and "A Small House with Lots of Room in It," for
less than $6,000. In practice, most of Wright's clients were wealthy suburban
businessmen and his designs usually ended up costing much more than they
had intended to spend, especially when Wright involved such colleagues as
sculptor Richard Bock and artist George Niedecken in the overall plan. However, the results were so pleasing and unusual that many clients gave Wright a

BELOW: *Wright's design "A Home in a Prairie Town" was published in the* Ladies' Home Journal *in 1901. This introduced Wright's Prairie House style and brought him national attention.*

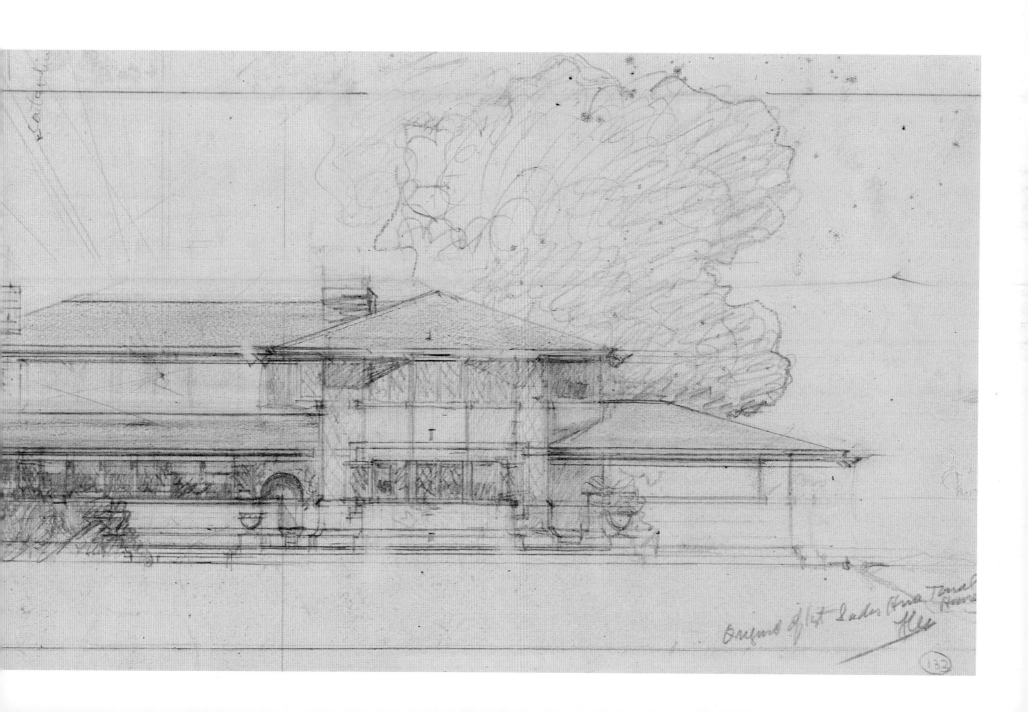

BELOW: *Wright's Unity Temple, Oak Park, Illinois, 1904.*

free hand and were glad they had done so. This was the case with the Ward W. Willits House, built in Highland Park, Illinois, in 1901, and with the 1902 design for the William E. Martin House in Oak Park. When Martin's brother, businessman Darwin D. Martin of Buffalo, New York, commissioned a house from Wright the results were less satisfactory because Martin and his wife demanded incessant changes in the design.

In the mid-1890s Wright had designed two apartment buildings for downtown Chicago: the elegant Robert W. Roloson Apartments and the Francisco Terrace Apartments, designed as low-cost housing for working-class families. The Roloson Apartments were a series of steeply gabled identical town houses, or row houses, which employed the mezzanine principle. Rooms at the front of the house are on a different level than those at the back, for optimum use of the available space for various living functions. This was a prototype of the ''zoned house'' concept that Wright would return to time and again. Francisco Terrace had a visual relationship to the Larkin Company Administration Building in Buffalo, which was commissioned in 1903 by Darwin D. Martin. Both buildings effectively turned their backs on the city, looking inward to a large central court. At the corners of these buildings were large towers containing stairways and utilities. Access to Francisco Terrace was through a large ornamental arch, decorated in the Sullivanesque style with a pattern of foliage. The Larkin Company Building had no outside ornamentation, apart from several pylons and finials that looked quite incongruous in Buffalo's gritty factory district. Inside, the fortresslike building consisted of tiers of galleries rising over a skylighted central atrium in which Larkin employees conducted their business of filling mail orders, supervised from the galleries by management. Wright also undertook to design the metal office furniture for the building, whose innovations included the first commercial use of plate glass and air conditioning.

Wright's first ecclesiastical commission came from the Unitarian congregation at Oak Park, of which he was a member. When its church burned down, Wright was chosen to design the building that became famous as Unity Temple. Its stark walls of poured concrete, on the stylobate foundation that characterized his houses, rose higher every day, to the wonder of the congregation and all of Oak Park. It was like no church they had ever seen before. The upper story was pierced by windows between squarish, pre-Columbian-looking columns and a heavy slab roof at various levels jutted out over the

BELOW: *All that remains of the Francisco Terrace Apartments, built in Chicago in 1895, is the imposing entrance arch, which was dismantled and reconstructed on Euclid Place, Oak Park, in 1977.*

severe facade. As in the Larkin Company Building, massive towers at each corner emphasized the uncompromising lines of the building. The interior was a study in the language of free-flowing space for the purposes of worship and fellowship (Wright called the church's social hall "the good-time place"). The Unitarians were both bewildered and pleased by their new home, which still stands.

The years between 1905 and 1909 saw Wright's Prairie House style fully realized in a series of outstanding designs, including that of the Avery Coonley House in Riverside, Illinois; the F. F. Tomek House, also in Riverside; and the Frederick C. Robie House in Chicago, generally considered the culmination of this style. Built of brown brick with stone trim, the Robie House is a testament to Wright's evolving concept of residential architecture. The facade is almost featureless, apart from the cantilevered roof that wings out more than twenty feet at one level. The south-facing "front" of the house and its many balconies overlook the enclosed garden and adjacent trees. Since nature was in short supply on this city lot, outdoor living was designed for privacy on sheltered porches and terraces. The interior is an unbroken flow of space on the ground floor, where a great chimney breast serves to define what traditional houses divide into living room, dining room, and library. Sleeping quarters are in the enclosed gallery, or belvedere, for privacy, and the carriage house of former days was replaced by a modern garage, with servants' quarters above. Characteristic of Wright is the unobtrusive entrance, tucked away so as to foster a sense of expectation about the interior and to reinforce the separation between the house and the world outside.

Implicit in Wright's designs for the Prairie House, and the Usonian House that succeeded it, was an ideal formed from his studies of Jefferson, Thoreau, and Emerson and deeply influenced by Louis Sullivan's views on urban architecture suitable to a democracy. Individual freedom and autonomy should prevail over what Wright called "the mobocracy." Towns and cities should be planned for the maximum benefit of their citizens, in terms of aesthetics, space, transportation, and communication. These concepts were utopian, and thus unrealizable on a massive scale, but the "organic society" was inseparable from Wright's organic architecture, which transcended Sullivan in affirming that "form and function are one."

Wright's enthusiasm, and the charismatic effect he had on his clients, resulted in a growing appreciation for what he would later call "the natural

ABOVE: *An interior view through the central atrium of the Larkin Company Administration Building. The Larkin Building, built in 1903 in Buffalo, New York, was demolished in 1949-50.*

OPPOSITE: *The Frederick C. Robie House in Chicago, Illinois. Designed in 1906, it is the best known of all Wright's houses in the Prairie style.*

house." As Brendan Gill writes in his outstanding biography of Wright, *Many Masks*, published by G. P. Putnam's Sons in 1987:

> If the Prairie House had little to do with an actual prairie, it had a great deal
> to do with how Wright believed people should live, not only as members
> of a family, but as citizens of a democracy. . . . Over the years, he managed
> to convince many people that his wide-eaved low roofs and massive chim-
> neys, his open porches and garden walls running out from the house
> proper in order to marry it to the ground, were outward and visible signs
> of the principles upon which the nation was founded. It was these princi-
> ples that he saw his floor plans as reflecting: rooms opened into one
> another without the usual peremptory boundaries of walls and doors, and
> a family was united by sharing spaces as well as activities.

In 1909 Wright made a decisive break with his life and career by going off to Europe with the wife of an Oak Park client. He had formed an attachment to Mamah Borthwick Cheney when he supervised the construction of her house, and grown increasingly disenchanted with the responsibilities and irritations of domestic life with Catherine and their six children. An offer by German publisher Ernst Wasmuth to publish a complete monograph of his work was the catalyst for his flight from Oak Park, where shock waves resounded throughout his long absence in Germany and Italy. When he returned with his companion in 1911, there was no possibility of resuming his former suburban life. He acquired property in the ancestral stronghold at Spring Green, Wisconsin, and began work on the rural estate he called Taliesin, from the Welsh for "shining brow."

Now more than forty years old, Wright retained his lifelong habit of getting deeply into debt. Formerly, he had blamed his precarious financial state on his large family, but the fact was that he had a passion for Japanese prints, stylish cars, grand pianos, and well-tailored clothes that cost far more than his daily domestic expenses. "Take care of the luxuries," he said airily, "and the necessities will take care of themselves." The handsome, rambling house that grew up on the hillside in Spring Green was a fresh source of expenditures that seemed unending. He thought of opening an office in Chicago but, as before, most of his work was done in the home studio at Taliesin. New projects such as the flamboyant Midway Gardens, an extensive Chicago

RIGHT: *Wright's country house and studio, Taliesin, built in 1911, in Spring Green, Wisconsin. Over the years Taliesin became one of the best known and most visited residences in the United States.*

recreational complex, and an invitation from the Japanese to design an Imperial Hotel grander than the German-built original in Tokyo, provided several years of feverish occupation.

The publication of the Wasmuth monograph, *Ausgeführte Bauten und Entwürfe von Frank Lloyd Wright*, and his travels in Europe between 1909 and 1911, made Wright's name widely known in international architecture. In Vienna he was compared to Joseph Maria Olbrich, who had designed the Secession Building to provide exhibition space for the *Kunst Haus* artists who were attracting so much attention at the time. Characteristically, Wright denied any debt to Olbrich, who was his own age, but the influence of the anticlassical Secessionist Building is clear in both the Larkin Building and Unity Temple. Similarly, he claimed that his work owed nothing to Japanese architecture, even though Japanese elements appeared in his designs as early as the 1890s and increased after his first visit to the Far East. He did acknowledge how much he had learned from the Japanese print, on which he became an authority. His own large collection was eventually willed to museums.

In 1914 Wright's personal and professional life was disrupted by a tragedy that would affect him for decades. Mamah Cheney, who had been divorced by her husband in 1911 on grounds of desertion, had her two children at Taliesin for a visit in August 1914 when a servant ran amok and killed seven people. He burned the family living quarters during the rampage and attempted suicide by poison, to which he succumbed weeks later in jail. Among the dead at Taliesin were Mamah Cheney and both her children, the son of craftsman William Weston, who saved much of the complex from the fire, and three apprentices and workmen. Wright was in Chicago, working on the Midway Gardens project, when he received the news.

Over the next several years Wright nearly bankrupted himself in the effort to rebuild Taliesin. His principal prospect of income was the $300,000 fee offered by the Japanese for the Imperial Hotel project. Wright sailed for Tokyo in December 1916. With him was Miriam Noel, an unstable woman with an artistic background with whom he would live unhappily for the next seven years and whom he would eventually marry, after his divorce from Catherine Wright.

Most of Wright's time between 1915 and 1922 was occupied with the design and construction of the massive hotel, for which he also provided all the furnishings down to the table settings and several miles of carpeting, hand-

OPPOSITE: *The Imperial Hotel in Tokyo, Japan, was designed and built between 1915 and 1922. Though the massive hotel was demolished in 1968, part of the lobby was reconstructed at Meiji Mura Park in Nagoya.*

RIGHT: *Miriam Noel was Wright's second wife.*

RIGHT: *Wright's work was compared to that of Josef Maria Olbrich (1867-1908). Here is Olbrich's design for Hochzeitsturm, 1907-08.*

woven in China to his designs. He devised an elaborate foundation that enabled the hotel to survive the great earthquake of 1923 and employed Japanese methods of masonry along with the innovative use of carved lava to dress the brickwork. The roof was of lightweight copper rather than the traditional heavy tiles, which rained into the streets during Japan's frequent earthquakes with fatal results.

The Imperial Hotel was atypical of anything Wright had done, or would do, but it was an imposing structure and widely considered a success, despite its grandiosity. Throughout this period Wright made trips to the Midwest and California where, in 1917, he designed the famous Hollyhock House in Los Angeles for actress Aline Barnsdall. This house, too, was a radical break from the past, imposing itself on its hilltop site like a Mayan monolith, studded with angular poured-concrete "flowers" that had little to do with either nature or art.

During this same period Wright worked with Milwaukee's Arthur Richards Company on the use of precut lumber for inexpensive prefabricated housing that would combine new technology with optimum use of natural materials. This American Readicut system was the product of Wright's commitment to attractive but affordable housing for the average citizen, articulated as early as 1901 in his famous lecture at Chicago's Hull House, "The Art and Craft of the Machine."

Another development of the early 1920s was the concrete-block house, seven of which were built for California clients. Wright had long been intrigued by the potential of concrete, generally considered a useful but homely building material. In 1923 he devised a way to impose geometric patterns on precast concrete blocks, which could be bound together at the building site with steel tie rods and poured concrete. The first and most striking use of this "textile-block" system was the house built in a Pasadena ravine for Mrs. George Millard. This compact, richly decorated house, called La Miniatura, became more beautiful with time, as tropical vines and foliage plants grew up to cover the pierced and patterned blocks that formed it. The effect was that of a rich mosaic, inside and out, as the blocks were decorated on both sides. Other structures in this mode, all built in or near Los Angeles, where Wright had maintained an office since 1917, were the Ennis, Freeman, and Storer houses. In 1929 Wright used alternating concrete and glass blocks to design a large house for his cousin Richard Lloyd Jones in Tulsa, Oklahoma.

BELOW: *Hollyhock (The Aline Barnsdall House) in Los Angeles, California, was built in 1917.*

RIGHT: *For La Miniatura (The Mrs. George Madison Millard House) in Pasadena, California, Wright used a new textile-block construction. The house was erected in 1923.*

Many promising projects of the 1920s came to grief because of the lack of money to build them. One of these was a proposed resort complex for Chandler, Arizona, called San Marcos-in-the-Desert, which Wright began to work on in 1927 with the property owner. That winter he established Ocotilla Camp in the desert near Chandler as a working refuge from the bitter cold of Wisconsin. He had been invited to help design the Arizona Biltmore Hotel and Cottages in Phoenix that year, and this successful project led to other contacts in the Southwest. Unfortunately, the stock-market crash of 1929 ended the San Marcos project, which went into the drawing file with other unbuilt projects such as the Lake Tahoe Summer Colony proposed for Emerald Bay, California, in 1922. Wright called them his "office tragedies." But it was not unusual for him to go back to these designs even years later and rework them for another client. This was the case with the 1928 project for St. Mark's Tower in New York City, which was built decades later as the Price Company Tower in Bartlesville, Oklahoma.

There was little work to be done in the early 1930s, so Wright turned to writing and lecturing for income and to promulgate his ideas. In a 1931 lecture at New York City's New School for Social Research, he called for a reconsideration of the skyscraper, which he considered (reluctantly) "the most typical product of the American civilization." Wright proposed that high-rise buildings should not crowd in upon each other as they did, but should occupy separate, parklike settings, widely spaced and easily accessible as both dwellings and workplaces. This proposal for decentralized cities would take form in the model for Broadacre City, a project built by Wright's apprentices at Taliesin for the 1935 Industrial Arts Exhibition at Rockefeller Center in Manhattan. The Broadacre City concept would occupy Wright for the rest of his life, and it became the point of departure for some of his masterworks, including the S. C. Johnson Administration Building in Racine, Wisconsin (1936), and the Hanna House (called Honeycomb House) in Palo Alto, California.

In 1932 Longmans, Green & Company published the first edition of Wright's *An Autobiography*, which stimulated new interest in his work, especially among young people who had considered him an eccentric elder statesman of architecture. Some of them came to Spring Green as paying apprentices and later worked with Wright on Taliesin West, his winter home in Scottsdale, Arizona, beginning in 1937. By this time, Wright had divorced Miriam Noel and married Olgivanna Milanov, a Montenegrin dancer who

SAN MARCOS   IN   THE

FOR Iº WELLINGTON AND RALPH CUDN

RIGHT AND RIGHT BELOW: *The unrealized plan for St. Mark's Tower on the Bowery, in New York, became the basis for the Price Company Tower in Bartlesville, Oklahoma. The St. Mark's plan was executed in 1928; the Price Tower was built in 1952.*

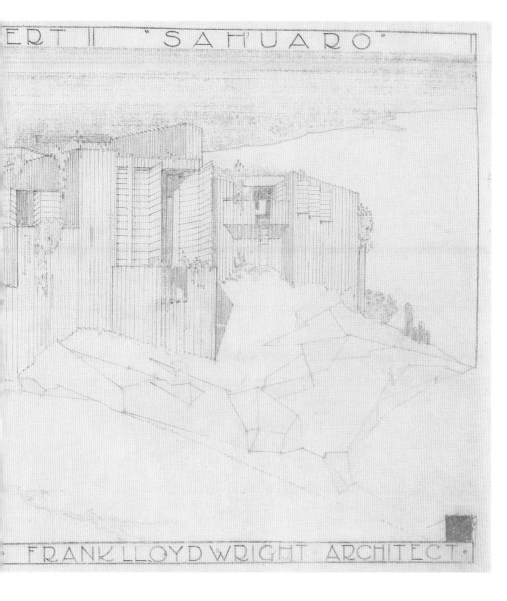

ERT II "SAHUARO"

FRANK LLOYD WRIGHT ARCHITECT

FIRST GROVP

N THE BOUWERIE. NEW YORK CITY. FRANK LLOYD WRIGHT ARCHITECT

had spent time at the Gurdjieff Institute in Fontainebleau. She relieved him of
many day-to-day problems and fostered the reverential – some would say
cultlike – attitude toward him on the part of many members of the Taliesin
Fellowship. As this circle grew, the Spring Green complex absorbed the
former Hillside Home School, which Wright had built for his aunts Nell and
Jane in 1903. The apprentices took care of the studio, house, and grounds,
while working on design projects with Wright. They also built and rebuilt the
beautiful complex at Taliesin West – a rambling structure of superimposed
geometrical forms constructed of desert rock with tentlike canvas roofing.

Wright had always been an outspoken critic of most other architects,
and this held true when his reputation revived and grew greater during the
1930s. When such younger American architects as Philip Johnson and Henry-
Russell Hitchcock coined the term International Style to describe the Euro-
pean architects they admired most – Le Corbusier, Gropius, Mies van der
Rohe – Wright belittled the style and announced that its proponents had
copied *him*. Now almost seventy years of age, he had embarked upon a whole
new career that would flourish into his nineties.

Probably Wright's best-known work is the beautiful house called Fallingwater in Mill Run, Pennsylvania. It was designed for department-store
owner and philanthropist Edgar J. Kaufmann, Sr., and his family in 1935. It
occupies a wooded site on a stream and waterfall in western Pennsylvania.
Photographs cannot do the house justice: it must be viewed from every angle,
like a sculpture, with its soaring cantilevered roofs and terraces, expanses of
mitered glass, rough-hewn rock, and total affinity with its setting. Other
notable works of the late 1930s are the Herbert F. Johnson House, called
Wingspread, at Wind Point, Wisconsin, and the first Usonian House, built for
– and with – Herbert and Katherine Jacobs in Madison, Wisconsin.

"Usonian" was one of Wright's memorable coined words, like "carport" and "textile block." It is generally believed to be an acronym for
"United States of North America," which accurately describes the endless
possibilities of this concept. Essentially, the Usonian House was intended to
be moderately priced, partially prefabricated, and constructed of wood, glass,
and brick under a slab roof. Wright described this simplified and scaled-down
version of the Prairie House in *The Natural House*, published in 1954. By this
time he had built dozens of Usonian Houses for clients all over the country,
each tailored to its site. There were five basic types of plan: rectangular; L- or

T-shaped, with one or more wings; "in-line," or single-block, with bedrooms at one end; hexagonal, like the Hanna House and the project for the Jester House in Palos Verdes, California; and a rectangular plan raised on masonry piers for steeply sloping sites. An example of this latter type is the striking George Sturges House in Brentwood Heights, California.

The house designed for publisher Ben Rebhuhn in Great Neck, New York, in 1937, is a widely admired example of the Usonian style. It is a two-story house with several level changes around a massive fireplace core. The bedroom wing projects above the garages, and the flat-roofed kitchen and dining area forms another wing, screened by built-in fixtures for displaying books and artwork. A two-story living area runs from the fireplace to huge windows on the garden. Glass walls and doors were a primary feature of the Usonian Houses, linking indoors and outdoors.

The Sidney Bazett House in Hillsborough, California (1939), is a small hexagonal plan with two wings at 60-degree angles enclosing the corner of the garden. The carport is linked to the guest house, and a balcony overlooks a steep drop on the southeast side. At the entryway, the floor level drops into a long living area with a glass wall to the garden on one side. At the fireplace the lines of cypress-paneled ceilings from three roof areas meet. There is a clear contrast between the "public zone" and the bedrooms, which are on a very small scale, with built-in storage and shower facilities.

The Pope-Leighey House, built in Falls Church, Virginia, is a rectangular plan with L-shaped wings. It was originally built around a shade-giving tulip tree and is unusual in having a five-step drop down into the living area, which looks out on both sides of the house. A long bookshelf/seating fixture faces north and the dining alcove, south.

The key to the informality and moderate cost of the Usonian House was the tightly designed service area, with utilities housed in a core of brickwork. The kitchen was laid out as efficiently as a ship's galley and its ceiling was carried up to clerestory windows that kept the workspace light and odor-free. There was usually one bathroom in the smaller Usonians, and basements were eliminated except for a small area designed to house fuel and laundry facilities. Heating was through radiant electrical coils built into the floor slab.

The Rose Pauson House in Phoenix, Arizona (1939), was built of desert stone on a small hill above the road. A stepped walkway up to the house went straight through it to emerge as a balcony at the far side overlooking the

RIGHT: *The 1939 George Sturges House, in Brentwood Heights, California, makes striking use of the cantilever principle.*

mountains in the distance. The two-story living room had a glass wall on the same view. Unfortunately, the Pauson House was destroyed by fire.

The early 1940s saw a moratorium on building as the nation fought World War II. Wright published a revised version of *An Autobiography* with Duell, Sloan & Pearce in 1943, but it was not until after the war that his ideas on modern housing became widely accepted. In essence, they had been formed very early in his career and modified through fifty years of social change, incessant work, and a gift for anticipating the needs of his times. He saw the future of architecture as an integration of nature with the potentiality of the machine for a more fully human civilization. In a 1936 article for the *Architects' Journal of London*, Wright restated this theme: "The proper use of the machine should be to make life more beautiful, more livable. No, not necessarily easier or quicker just to feed this American voracity which we call speed. If speed and destruction plus sanitation are to be the function of machinery among us, the machine will destroy us and its present idolatry will eventually defeat our attempt at a culture."

New forms came into being during the last decade of Wright's life, notably the spiral-ramp plan used for the David Wright House in Phoenix, the V. C. Morris Gift Shop in San Francisco, and the Solomon R. Guggenheim Museum in New York City. A number of ecclesiastical commissions resulted in houses of worship that were as revolutionary for their times as Unity Temple had been in the early 1900s. These included the Unitarian Church in Shorewood Hills, Wisconsin, which seems about to take flight from the earth; Temple Beth Sholom in Elkins Park, Pennsylvania, designed to symbolize Mount Sinai as a "moving mountain of light"; and the Annunciation Greek Orthodox Church in Wauwatosa, Wisconsin, which incorporated the arch and the cross central to the faith of this Christian community.

Wright's vision of "the city of broad acres" was never to materialize except in such fragments as the unbuilt projects for Point View Residence in Pittsburgh, Pennsylvania, and the Garden of Eden complex proposed for Baghdad, Iraq, in 1952. Elements of the utopian city were incorporated into the Marin County Civic Center in San Raphael, California, which broke ground in 1959, the year of Wright's death. However, the 300 or more buildings of his design still standing at that time gave their testimony to the immense energy and creativity of the architect and artisan who remains the single greatest influence on twentieth-century design in America.

RIGHT: *The plastic-domed Marin County Administration Building, which broke ground in 1959.*

RIGHT: *The David Wright House in Phoenix, Arizona. Wright built this circular house for his son in 1950; its wide ramp reflects Wright's simultaneous preoccupation with the Guggenheim Museum project, still far from completion.*

OVERLEAF: *Frank Lloyd Wright poses with his "future farm home" during a guest appearance on the television program "RFD Chicagoland", in the 1950s. The model was designed in the 1920s.*

THE PLATES

Frank Lloyd Wright Home and Studio,
1889-1909
Drafting Room
Oak Park, Illinois
Photo: Hedrich Blessing

OPPOSITE:
Frank Lloyd Wright Home and Studio,
1889-1909
Photo: Judith Bromley

OPPOSITE:
Frank Lloyd Wright Home and Studio,
1889-1909
Living Room
Oak Park, Illinois
Photo: Judith Bromley

Frank Lloyd Wright Home and Studio,
1889-1909
South Bedroom
Oak Park, Illinois
Photo: Judith Bromley

William H. Winslow House, 1893
River Forest, Illinois
Photo: © Ron Schramm

OPPOSITE:
William H. Winslow House, 1893
Drawing
Copyright © 1985 the Frank Lloyd
Wright Foundation

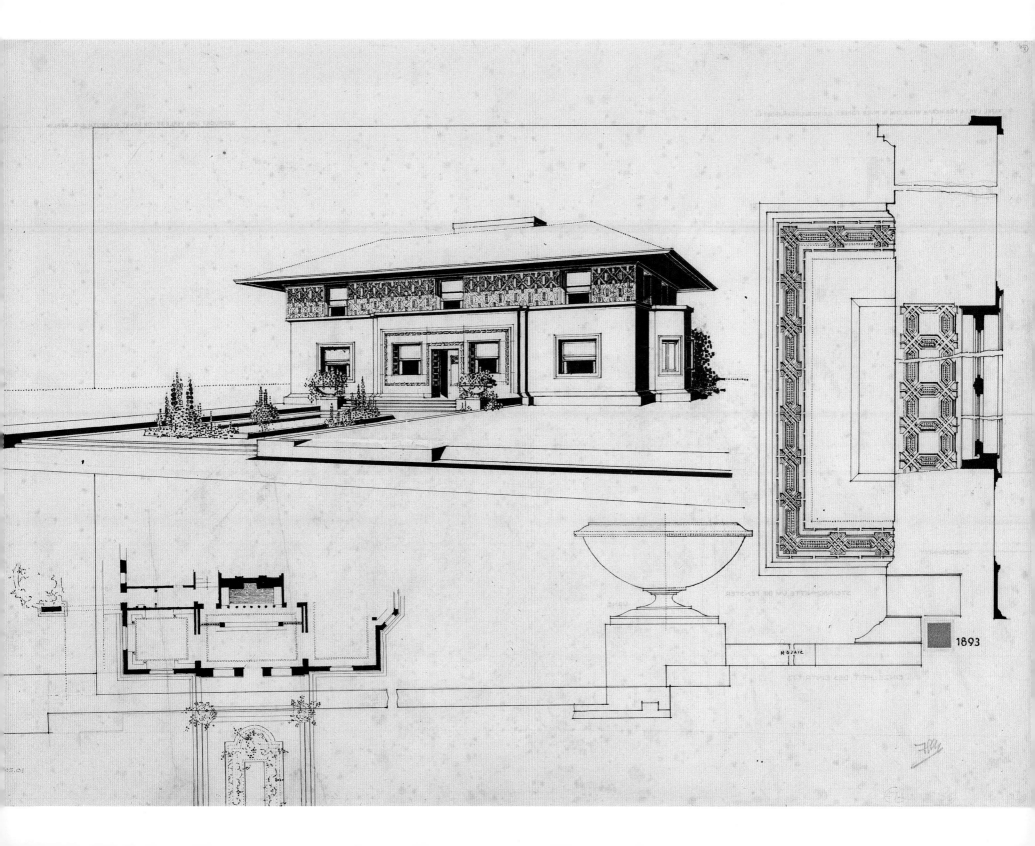

1893

Rollin Furbeck House, 1897
Oak Park, Illinois
Photo: © Ray F. Hillstrom Jr.

Rollin Furbeck House, 1897
Photo: © Ray F. Hillstrom Jr.

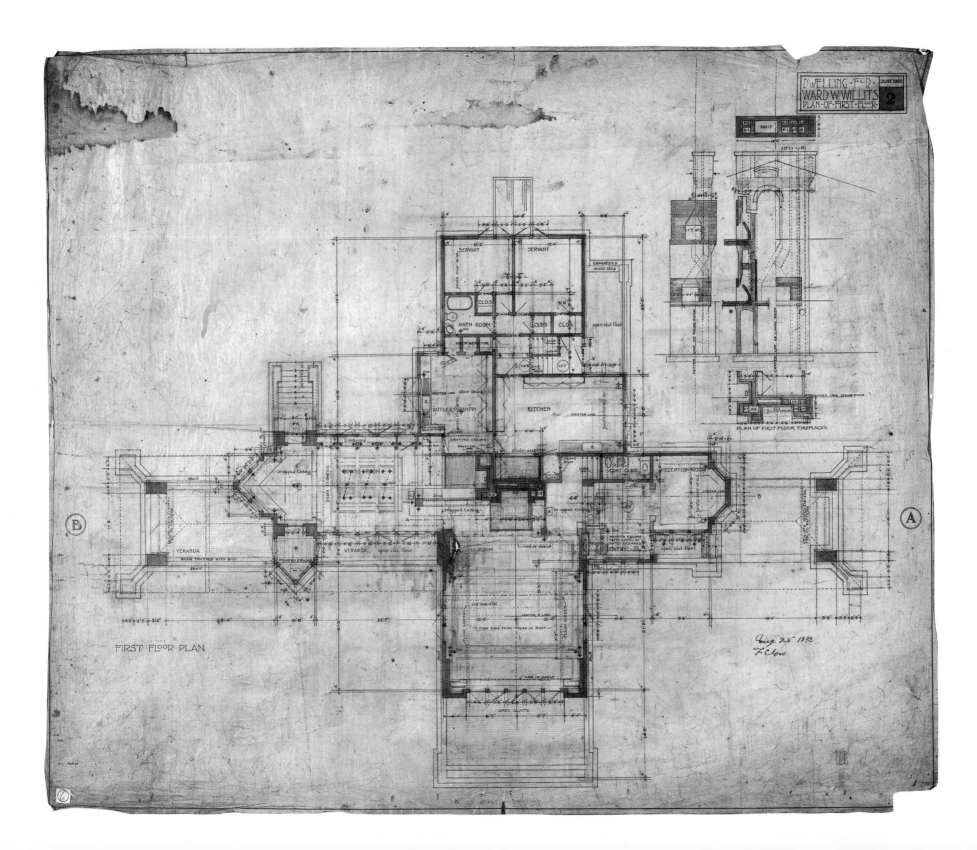

FIRST FLOOR PLAN

OPPOSITE:
Ward W. Willits House, 1901
Plan
Highland Park, Illinois
© courtesy the Frank Lloyd Wright
Archives

Ward W. Willits House, 1901
Photo: © 1992 Ron Schramm

William E. Martin House, 1902
Oak Park, Illinois
Photo: Thomas A. Heinz

William E. Martin House, 1902
Living Room
Photo: Thomas A. Heinz

LEFT:
Arthur Heurtley House, 1902
Oak Park, Illinois
Photo: Balthazar Korab

Reclining Arm Chair, c. 1902
designed for the Arthur Heurtley House
Photo: Domino's Pizza Collection

Susan Lawrence Dana House, 1902
Springfield, Illinois
Photo: Thomas A. Heinz
Courtesy: The Illinois Historic
Preservation Agency

Susan Lawrence Dana House, 1902
Gallery
Photo: Judith Bromley
Courtesy: The Illinois Historic
Preservation Agency

Unity Temple, 1904
Oak Park, Illinois
Photo: © Balthazar Korab

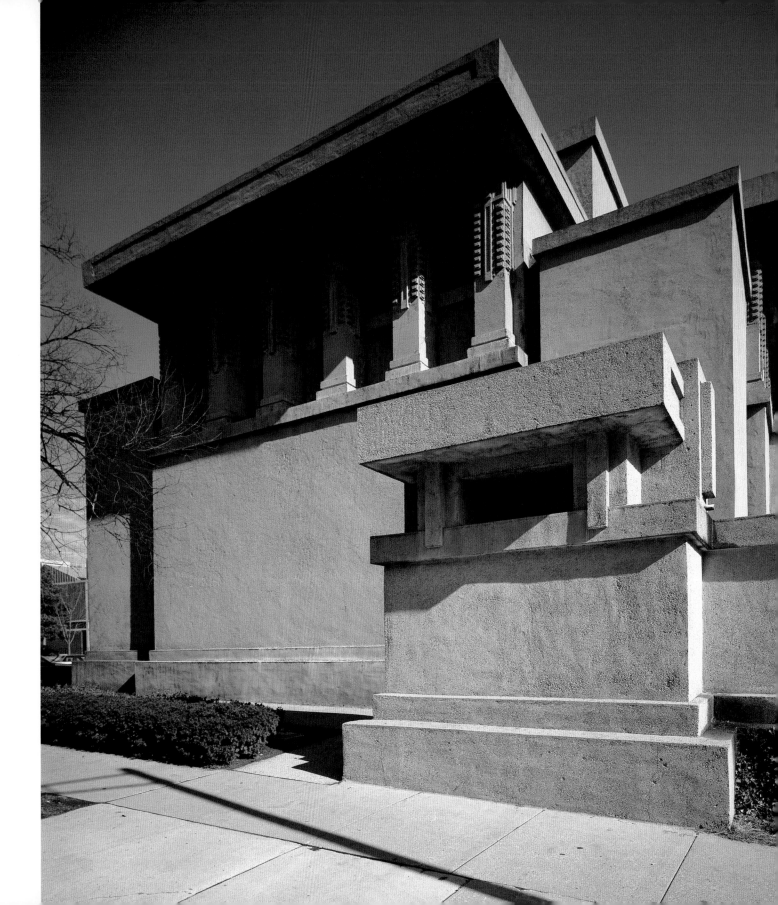

OPPOSITE:
Darwin D. Martin House, 1904
Living Room
Buffalo, New York
Photo: Thomas A. Heinz

Darwin D. Martin House, 1904
Photo: © Balthazar Korab

Frederick C. Robie House, 1906
Exterior detail
Chicago, Illinois
Photo: © Balthazar Korab

RIGHT:
Frederick C. Robie House, 1906
Photo: © Balthazar Korab

Meyer May House, 1908
Living Room
Photo: © Balthazar Korab

Meyer May House, 1908
Grand Rapids, Michigan
Photo: courtesy of Steelcase, Inc.

LEFT:
Taliesin, 1911-1959
Spring Green, Wisconsin
Photo: Thomas A. Heinz

RIGHT:
Taliesin, 1911-1959
Garden Steps
Photo: © Balthazar Korab

Taliesin, 1911-1959
Living Room
Photo: Thomas A. Heinz

OPPOSITE:
Avery Coonley Playhouse, 1912
Interior
Riverside, Illinois
Photo: Judith Bromley

Child's Side Chair
designed for the Coonley Playhouse
Photo: Domino's Pizza Collection

OPPOSITE:
Midway Gardens, 1913
(demolished 1929)
Chicago, Illinois
Photo: Domino's Pizza Collection

LEFT:
Plates designed for Midway Gardens
Photo: Domino's Pizza Collection

ABOVE:
Midway Gardens, 1913
Interior
Photo: Domino's Pizza Collection

Imperial Hotel, 1915-22
(demolished 1968)
Tokyo, Japan
Photo: Domino's Pizza Collection

OPPOSITE:
Imperial Hotel, 1915-22
Lobby Interior
Photo: Domino's Pizza Collection

OPPOSITE:
Hollyhock House, 1917
(Aline Barnsdall House)
Los Angeles, California
Photo: Tom Ploch

LEFT:
Lantern, c. 1920
designed for Hollyhock House
Photo: Domino's Pizza Collection

BELOW:
Hollyhock House, 1917
Photo: Thomas A. Heinz

OPPOSITE:
Mrs. George Madison Millard House,
1923
(La Miniatura)
Pasadena, California
Photo: John R. Bare

Charles Ennis House, 1923
Los Angeles, California
Photo: © Balthazar Korab

John Storer House, 1923
Hollywood, California
Photo: Tom Ploch

Arizona Biltmore, 1927
Phoenix, Arizona
Photo: © Balthazar Korab

Fallingwater, 1935
(Edgar J. Kaufmann, Sr. House)
Mill Run, Pennsylvania
Photo: Thomas A. Heinz, photographer
for The Western Pennsylvania
Conservancy

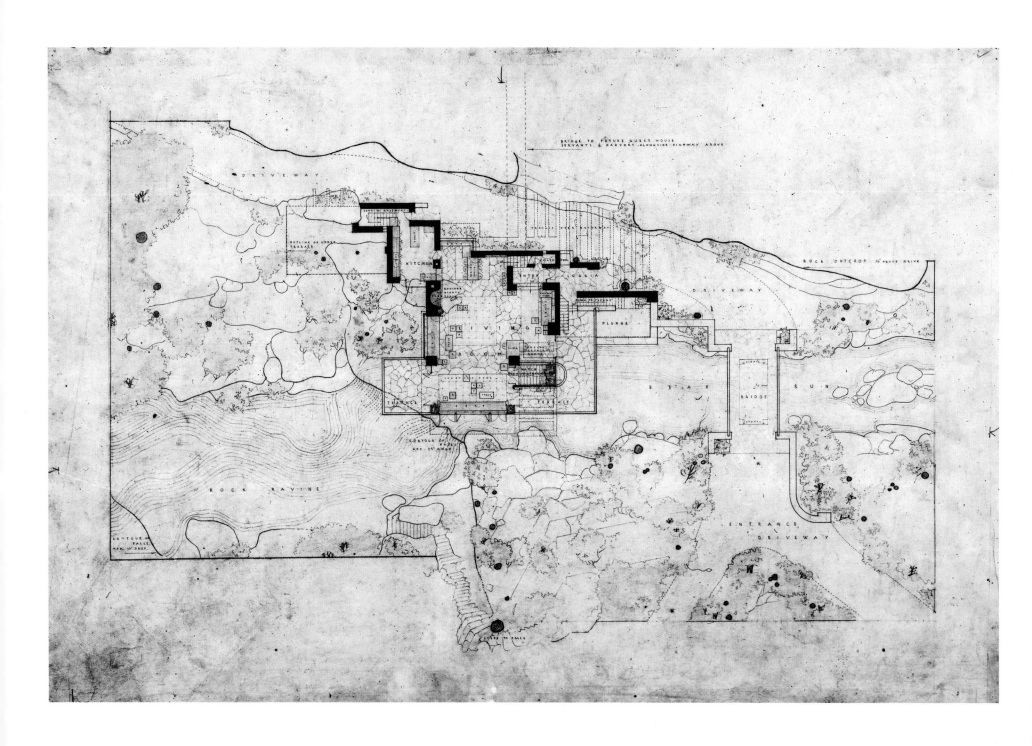

OPPOSITE:
Fallingwater, 1935
(Edgar J. Kaufmann, Sr. House)
Plan
Mill Run, Pennsylvania
© courtesy the Frank Lloyd Wright
Archives

Fallingwater, 1935
(Edgar J. Kaufmann, Sr. House)
Master Bedroom
Photo: Christopher Little

Fallingwater, 1935
(Edgar J. Kaufmann, Sr. House)
Mill Run, Pennsylvania
Photo: Thomas A. Heinz, photographer
for The Western Pennsylvania
Conservancy

OPPOSITE:
S. C. Johnson and Son
Administration Building, 1936;
and Research Tower, 1944
Racine, Wisconsin
Photo: Thomas A. Heinz

LEFT:
S. C. Johnson and Son
Administration Building, 1936
Interior of the Great Work Room
Photo: © Balthazar Korab

ABOVE:
S. C. Johnson and Son Administration
Building, 1936;
and Research Tower, 1944
Photo: © Balthazar Korab

OPPOSITE:
Paul R. Hanna House, 1936
(Honeycomb House)
Palo Alto, California
Photo: © Balthazar Korab

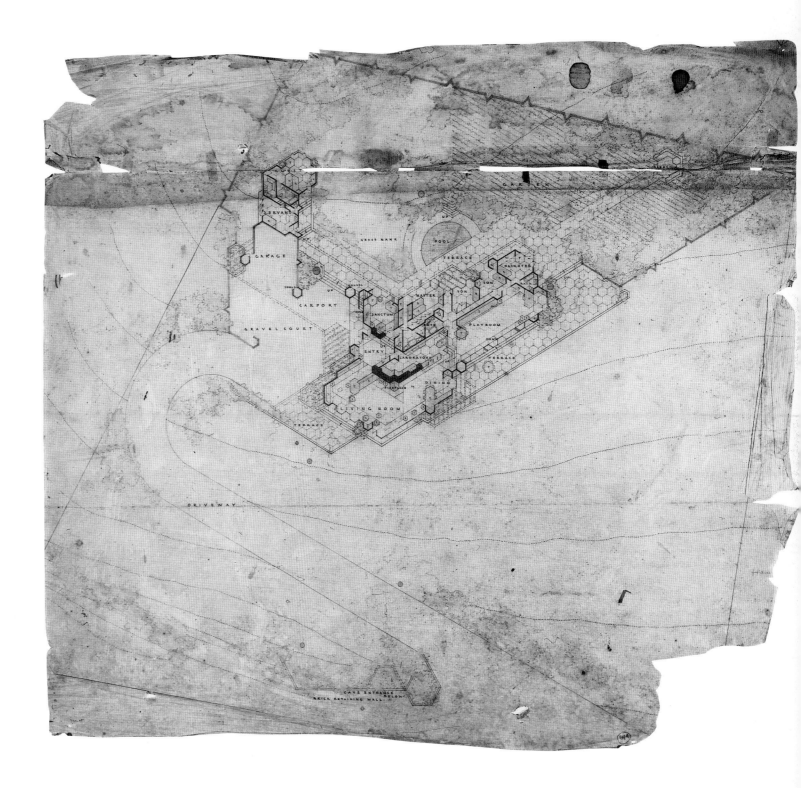

Paul R. Hanna House, 1936
Plan
© the Frank Lloyd Wright Archives

VEGETABLES

STUDY

SHOP

BEDROOM

GARDEN

BEDROOM

TERRACE

LINEN   DISHES   SEAT

DINING

DOWN   COOKING   LIVING ROOM

BATH   FIREPLACE

ENTRY   TABLE

BOOKSHELVES

CAR PORT
GRAVEL

LAWN

GRASS

BANK   GROUND COVER

GROUND   FLOOR   PLAN   HOUSE   FOR   HERBERT   JACOBS

WALK

SIDEWALK LINE

LOT LINE

CENTER   "   ROAD

OPPOSITE:
Herbert Jacobs House I, 1936
Plan
Madison, Wisconsin
© 1982 The Frank Lloyd Wright
Foundation

BELOW:
Herbert Jacobs House I, 1936
Drawing
© 1962 The Frank Lloyd Wright
Foundation

RIGHT:
Herbert Jacobs House I, 1936
Photo: Pedro E. Guerrero

HOUSE FOR HERBERT JACOBS

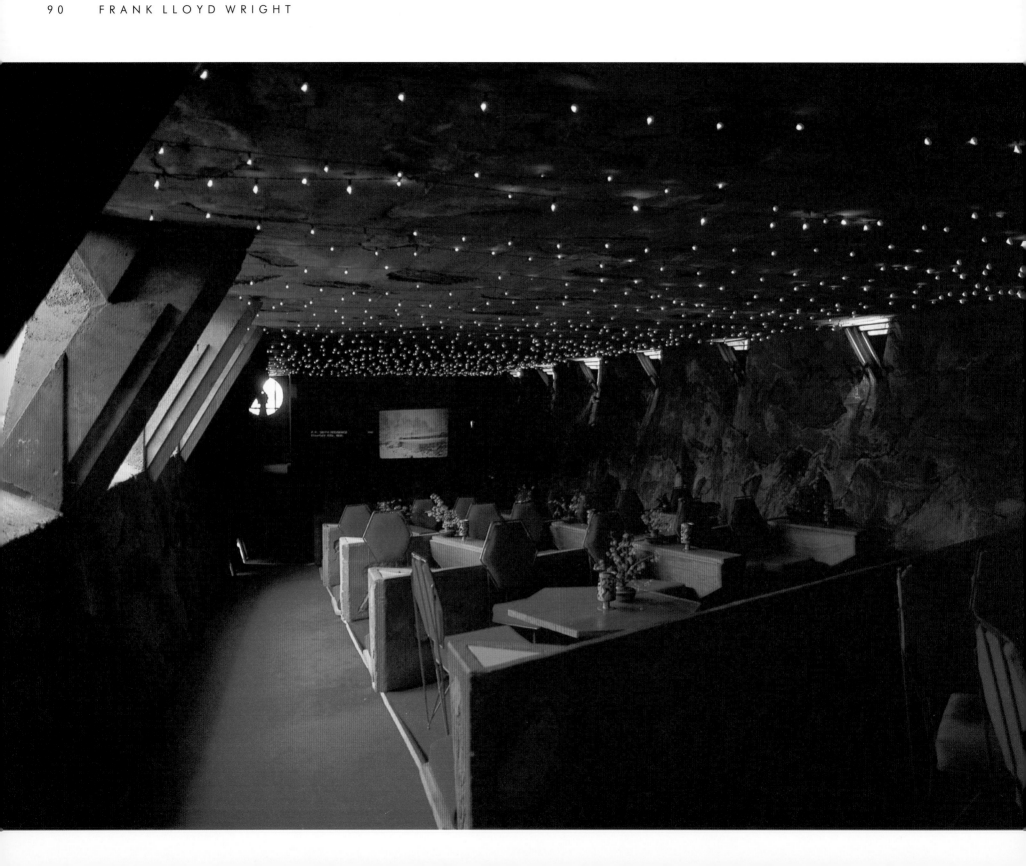

OPPOSITE:
Taliesin West, 1937-1959
Theater Interior
Scottsdale, Arizona
Photo: Thomas A. Heinz
Courtesy of the Frank Lloyd Wright
Foundation

RIGHT:
Taliesin West, 1937-1959
Photo: Thomas A. Heinz
Courtesy of the Frank Lloyd Wright
Foundation

RIGHT:
Taliesin West, 1937-1959
Drafting Room
Photo: Thomas A. Heinz
Courtesy of the Frank Lloyd Wright
Foundation

OPPOSITE:
Wingspread, 1937
(Herbert F. Johnson House)
Wind Point, Wisconsin
Photo: Thomas A. Heinz
Courtesy of The Johnson Foundation Inc.

Wingspread, 1937
(Herbert F. Johnson House)
Photo: Thomas A. Heinz
Courtesy of The Johnson Foundation Inc.

OPPOSITE:
Wingspread, 1937
(Herbert F. Johnson House)
Interior of the core "Wigwam"
Wind Point, Wisconsin
Photo: Thomas A. Heinz
Courtesy of The Johnson Foundation Inc.

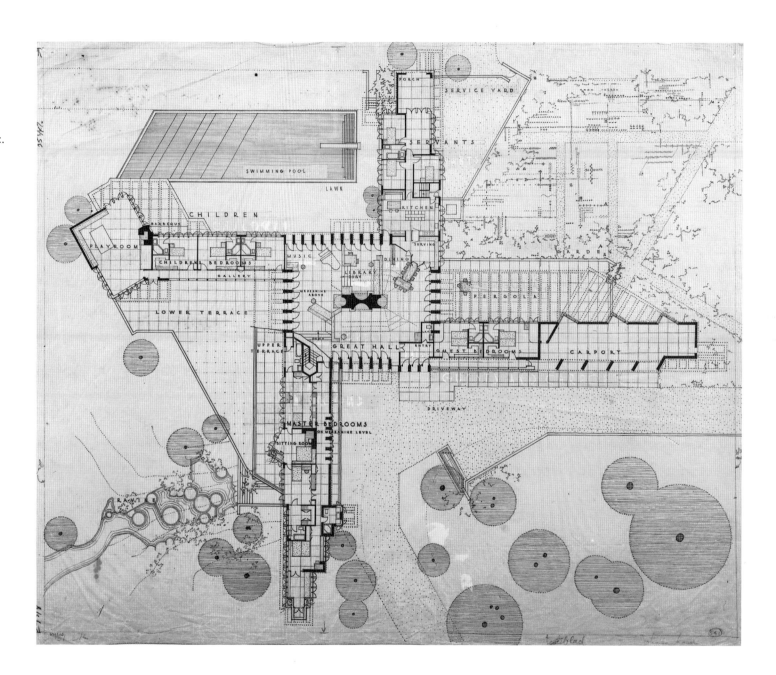

Wingspread, 1937
(Herbert F. Johnson House)
Plan
Copyright © 1955 The Frank Lloyd
Wright Foundation

Florida Southern College, 1938
Interior of Annie Pfeiffer Chapel
Lakeland, Florida
Photo courtesy of Florida Southern
College (FSC)

OPPOSITE:
Florida Southern College, 1938
Campus and exterior view of the chapel
Photo courtesy of Florida Southern
College (FSC)

Goetsch-Winkler House, 1939
Exterior detail
Okemos, Michigan
Photo: © Balthazar Korab

Goetsch-Winkler House, 1939
Photo: © Balthazar Korab

Lloyd Lewis House, 1939
Exterior detail
Libertyville, Illinois
Photo: © 1992 Ron Schramm

OPPOSITE:
Lloyd Lewis House, 1939
Photo: © 1992 Ron Schramm

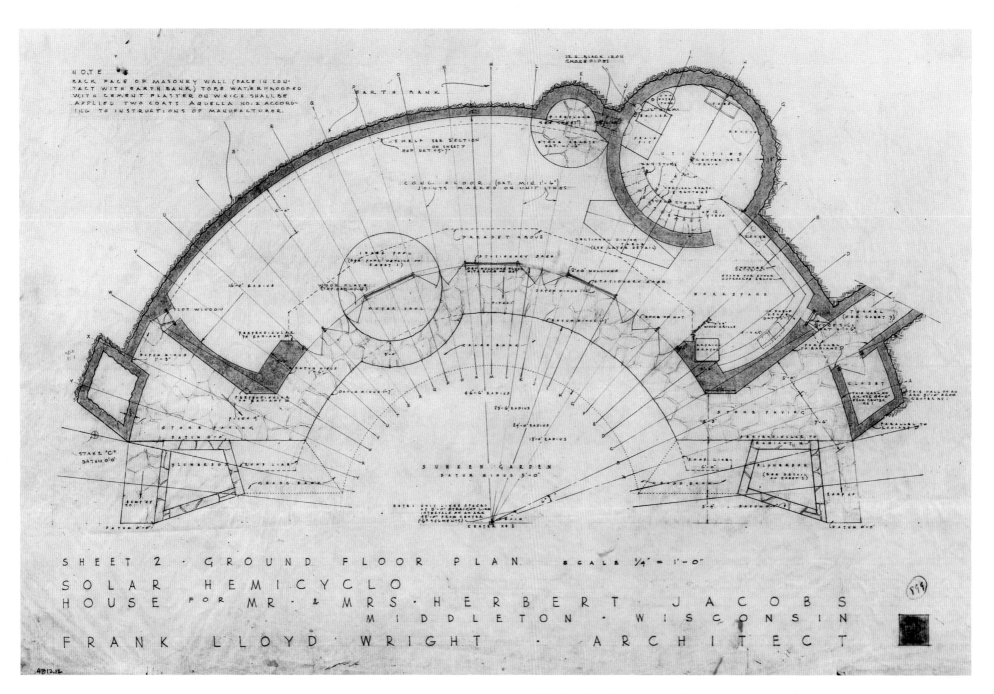

SHEET 2 · GROUND FLOOR PLAN   SCALE ¼" = 1'-0"
SOLAR HEMICYCLO
HOUSE FOR MR · & MRS · HERBERT · JACOBS
MIDDLETON · WISCONSIN
FRANK LLOYD WRIGHT · ARCHITECT

Herbert Jacobs House II, 1943
Plan
Middleton, Wisconsin
Copyright © 1982 The Frank Lloyd
Wright Foundation

OPPOSITE:
Melvyn Maxwell Smith House, 1946
Bloomfield Hills, Michigan
Photo: © Balthazar Korab

Melvyn Maxwell Smith House, 1946
Interior
Photo: © Balthazar Korab

Unitarian Church, 1947
Shorewood Hills, Wisconsin
Photo: Thomas A. Heinz

The V. C. Morris Gift Shop, 1948
San Francisco, California
Copyright © 1993 Marco P. Zecchin/
Image Center

Sol Friedman House, 1948
(Usonia Homes Cooperative)
Pleasantville, New York
Ezra Stoller © ESTO

RIGHT:
Sol Friedman House, 1948
(Usonia Homes Cooperative)
Carport
Ezra Stoller © ESTO

William Palmer House, 1950
Ann Arbor, Michigan
Photo: © Balthazar Korab

OVERLEAF:
William Palmer House, 1950
Living Room
Photo: © Balthazar Korab

Crescent Opera Civic Auditorium, 1952
Baghdad, Iraq
Drawing
Copyright © 1958 The Frank Lloyd
Wright Foundation

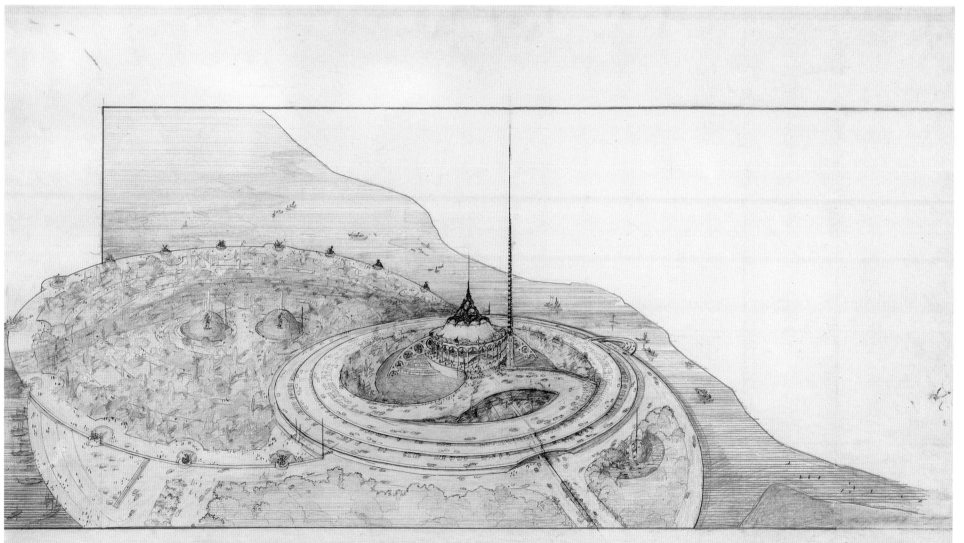

CRESCENT OPERA, CIVIC AUDITORIUM. GARDEN OF EDEN
PLAN FOR GREATER BAGHDAD
FRANK LLOYD WRIGHT ARCHITECT

Price Company Tower, 1952
(mural)
Bartlesville, Oklahoma
Courtesy The Phillips Petroleum
Company

RIGHT:
Price Company Tower, 1952
Courtesy The Phillips Petroleum
Company

BELOW:
Side Chair designed for the Price Tower
Photo: Domino's Pizza Collection

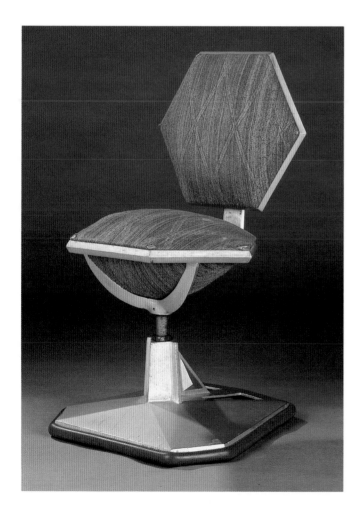

VIEW FROM NORTHEAST
POINT VIEW RESIDENCES
FOR THE EDGAR J. KAUFMANN CHARITABLE TRUST
FRANK LLOYD WRIGHT   ARCHITECT

Temple Beth Sholom, 1954
Elkins Park, Pennsylvania
Photo: Thomas A. Heinz

John L. Rayward House, 1955
(Tirranna)
New Canaan, Connecticut
Peter Aaron © ESTO

John L. Rayward House, 1955
(Tirranna)
Dining Room
New Canaan, Connecticut
Peter Aaron © ESTO

OPPOSITE:
John L. Rayward House, 1955
(Tirranna)
Living Room
Peter Aaron © ESTO

OPPOSITE:
Annunciation Greek Orthodox Church,
1956
Wauwatosa, Wisconsin
Photo: © Balthazar Korab

Annunciation Greek Orthodox Church,
1956
Interior
Photo: © Balthazar Korab

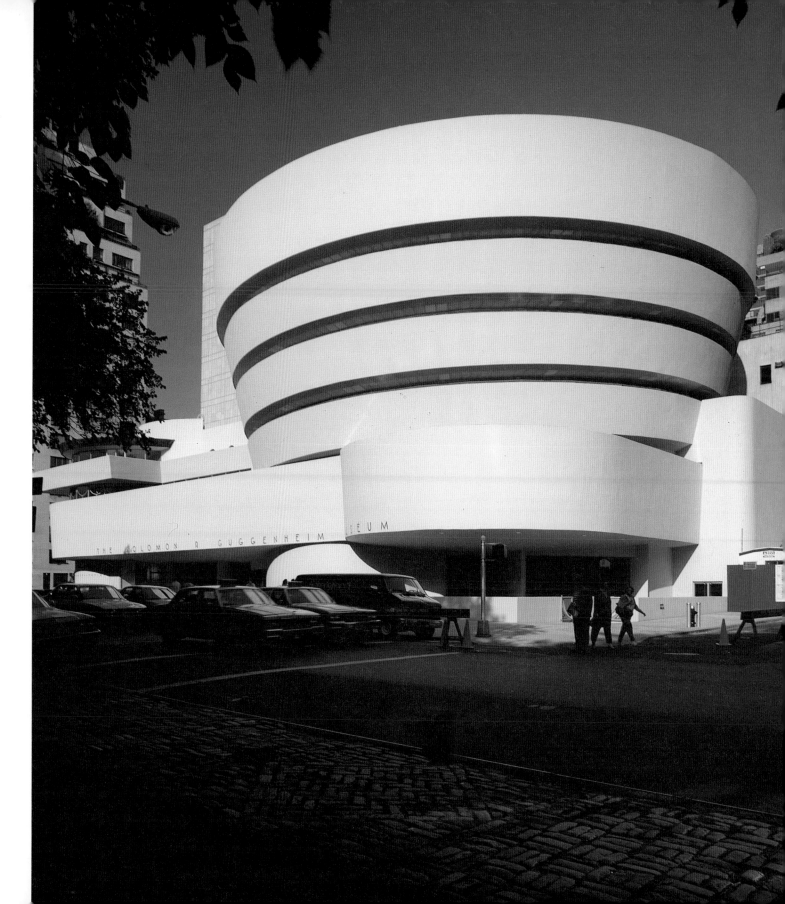

Solomon R. Guggenheim Museum, 1956
Photo: Thomas A. Heinz

Marin County Civic Center, 1957
San Raphael, California
Photo: Thomas A. Heinz

OPPOSITE:
Marin County Civic Center, 1957
Photo: © Balthazar Korab

LIST OF PLATES

Picture Credits
    John R. Bare © 1933: 23(right).
The Bettmann Archive: 8(both), 11(bottom).
British Architectural Library/RIBA: 10.
The Buffalo and Erie County Historical
    Society: 16.
The Courtauld Institute: 14-15.
Courtesy of The Frank Lloyd Wright
    Foundation: © 1986, 12-13, 21(top
    © 1942, 24-25; © 1962, 25(botton right),
    26, 27.
Courtesy of the Frank Lloyd Wright Home
    and Studio Foundation: 1, 6, 11(top).
© Pedro E. Guerrero: 28, 34-35.
Thomas A. Heinz: 9, 18-19, 20.
© Ray F. Hillstrom Jr.: 15(right).
© Balthazar Korab: 22-23.
Osterreichische Nationalbibliotek:
    21(bottom).
Courtesy of The Phillips Petroleum
    Company: 25(top).
Tom Ploch: 30-31.
© Ron Schramm: 17.
Ezra Stoller © ESTO: 29.
UPI/Bettmann Newsphotos: 7, 32-33, 36.

Acknowledgments
The publisher and author would like to thank
the following people who helped in the
preparation of this book: Design 23; Susan
Bernstein, the editor; and Elizabeth
Montgomery, the picture editor.